T0197453

COUNT US ALL IN TOGETHER
Poems for Children and Adults

Written and Illustrated by

Janice Peters Sean

Archway Publishing books may be ordered through booksellers or by contacting:

Archway Publishing
1663 Liberty Drive
Bloomington, IN 47403
www.archwaypublishing.com
1 (888) 242-5904

ISBN: 978-1-4808-5664-6 (sc)
ISBN: 978-1-4808-5663-9 (e)

Print information available on the last page.

Archway Publishing rev. date: 12/20/2017

Contents

This Book is dedicated to my mother
Beatrice Sophia Peters

CHAPTER

1

Count Us All In Together

Practicing counting is fun and exciting for preschool and kindergarten age children when it involves using clues from poems and playing Hide and Seek to explore nature, animals, stars and families. The corresponding picture is where the fun begins.

Way up high among the clouds,
Wet, fluffy, black and white,
Flew 1 swift bird, with all its might.

Beneath a canopy of green leafed trees,
Strolled 2 woolly Alpacas,
Named Elegance and Ease.

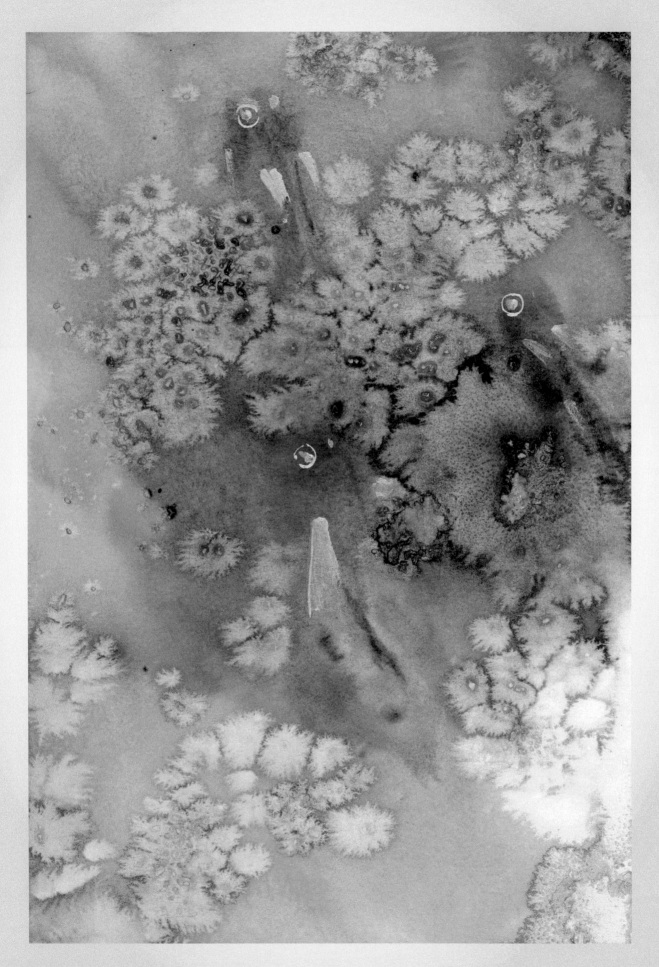

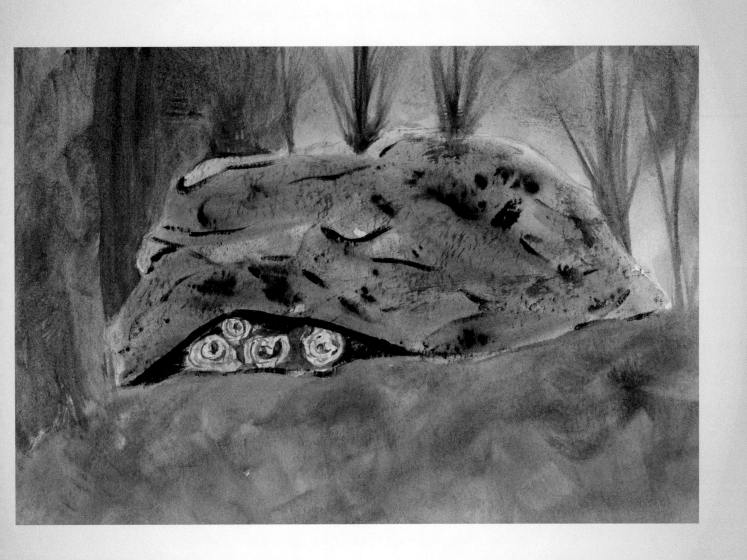

Above the clouds
In the darkness of night,
The Pleiades Sisters appear,
7 stars twinkling with light.

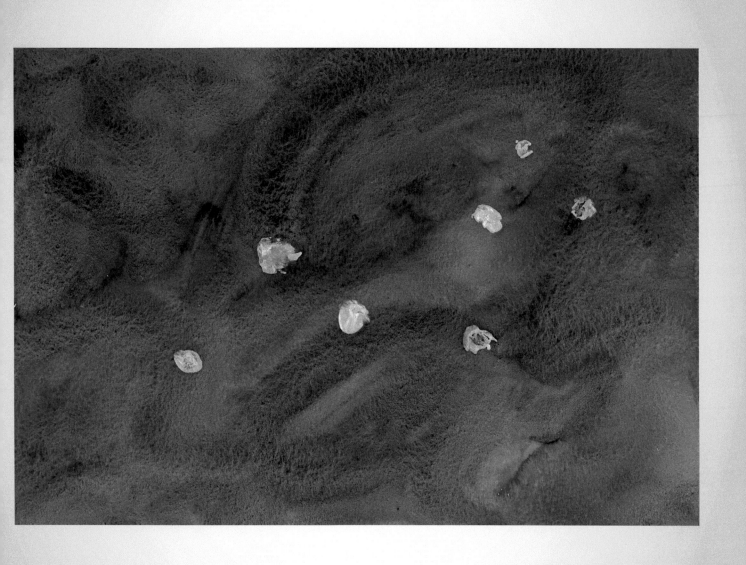

In Madison County the "A" trail extends,
Along the Blue Ridge Mountains,
And a river with 8 bends.

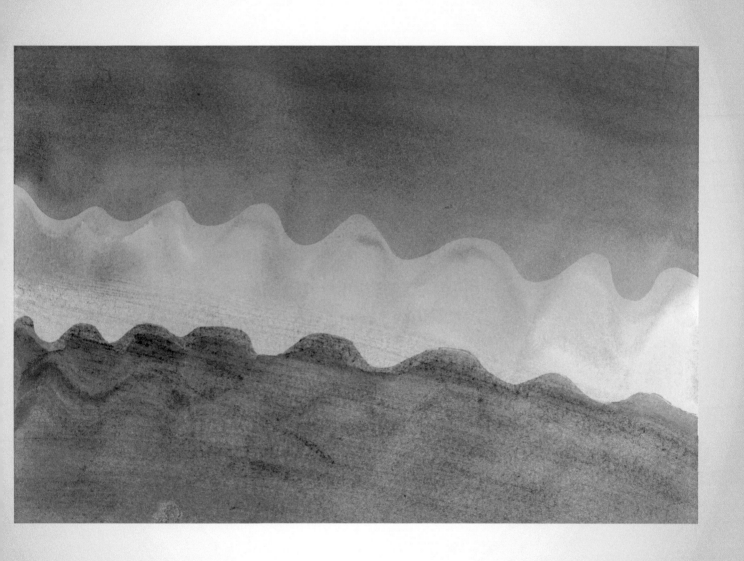

Circling our giant solar Sun
9 Planets race playing a game,
Just having fun.

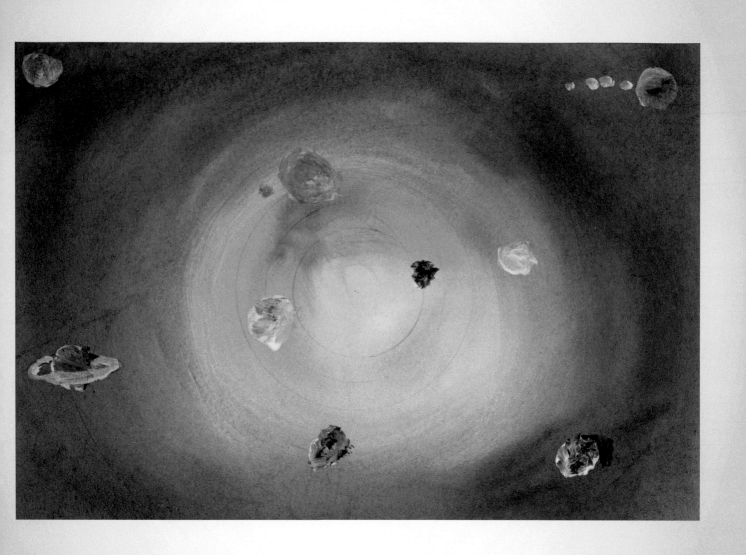

Falling freely, drifting down,
10 floating leaves turn to brown,
Resembling a palette an artist found.

Like all amusing things,
This poem here ends.
But you have the option
To count beyond tens.

CHAPTER
2
Life's Ebb And Flow –
Poems For All Ages

Why read a poem?

Just as children look for clues to hidden items while playing Hide and Seek. Likewise, navigating life's every day events can be eased by reading a poem which gives clues to what we are experiencing. Poetry addresses our sentient moods. Poetry forces us to examine our own mind-sets and reactions. It gives us hope when we realize that others share our angst and we are not alone. The corresponding pictures which accompany each poem in this collection are the author's response to the mood and tone of the poem. The fun is matching <u>your</u> mood to the abstract picture. For example, the first poem "Life's Ebb and Flow" depicts a cracked bowl. The cracks appear to be roads. Then you spot the two red arrows – pointing in and pointing out. The red arrows indicate that there is a way out of the chaos of a cracked situation.

Life's Ebb And Flow

Daily life is like a string of beads.

We hope for pearls and diamonds,

Jade, opal, sapphire and gold.

We yearn for constant good friends,

Loving family, devoted children.

We strive for wealth to provide necessities,

And added enjoyment, and education.

We cultivate ourselves to be compassionate,

Caring, enduring and content.

But some strings of beads are artificial,

Constructed faulty and frail:

Wax that melts

Glass that breaks

Wood that splinters

Stones that grind into dust.

We contemplate our beads at end of day,

And wonder why and how such change occurs.

Some days are congenial

Some days are banal.

How do we cope with disillusionments, cracked

friendships, forgotten promises?

How can we cope with the natural give and take of life,

Accepting its uneven flow?

Why, When, Because

Why drink a bottle of wine when the first sip will saturate the palate.
Why travel around the world when the first stranger
you meet expands your culture 100%
Why read a book of poems when understanding
the first one ignites enlightenment.
Why listen to hours of music when the first
measure sings the entire melody.
Why complete any task when the first tap of the
hammer is the beginning of the end.
BECAUSE not all stories are over
after we read the first line.

Rocking Chair Ride

Tilt sky-ward, surge for-ward

Tilt cloud-ward, slope ground-ward

Tilt star-ward, far-sight focus on a planet.

Pause, Hesitate, Wonder,

Seeing in all directions, dimensions.

Snap Awake.

Roll down-wards to the ground.

Near-sight focus on a plant.

Tilt sky-ward space-sight glancing.

See gliding birds forming smoggy cloud,

Worlds apart from "ward" to "ward",

Causing mind, body, soul to

Stop, Stay, Evaporate,

Letting free the knowing that all are part of

Ebb and Flow

Continuous cycles,

Come and Go.

It's A Periwinkle Morning

The mist is thick and dense,
Shaded whimsically soft pinks
And mauve,
Multi-dimensional.
The illusion is that this misty world
Would support me as I walked into it.
The illusion is that I could travel through it,
And over the mountain.
The illusion is that I could float carelessly,
Somersaulting in all directions.
Oh, what spirits would embrace me!
My soul would float unobstructed
In this incandescent atmosphere of
Puffy Breath.
In a dream-like state of consciousness,
I travel through time and space,
Faster than light
Accomplishing feats,
Acclaiming victories.
This is a periwinkle morning
Just before real dawn.

Will You Get Up

Oh, I wouldn't get up if I were you.

There's nothing here just morning dew,

Sodden deck, moldy table, frazzled chair,

Fungal trees, dripping leaves, misty air,

Just a trace of blue.

Oh, I mightn't get up if I were you.

There's nothing here just what grew.

Stalks green/red/orange/blue

Sky indigo blue showing through a bursted cloud,

Now waterless that minutes before drenched,

Drowned, poured down upon a pond,

Already full and surging through

A levee made of turtle dung.

Would I get up If I were you?

To see the minnows slip through the cracks

Of shimmering rocks, their fins

Aglow like petals where the rain

Alights softly clinging,

And a glimpse of sunshine begins to show,

And the hued arc across the land invites

Me through the door pane into the

Shiny warmth of noon.

Ah, I'd get up if I were you – Soon.

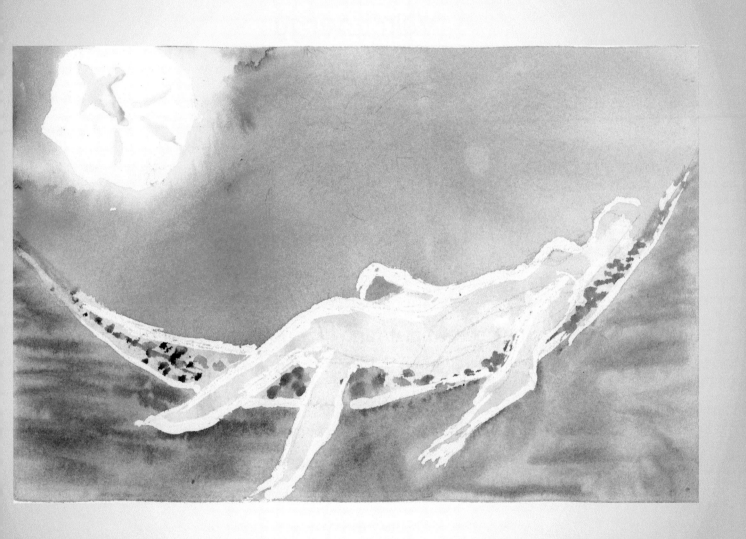

Vain Energy

Hard labor demonstrates
How resilient am I.
Moving large stones shows
How strong am I.
Hours of toil in the hot sun proves
How superior to others am I.
The magnificence of my garden displays
How creative am I.
To rest, contemplate and gaze upon the fields
Of wild flowers in blissful enjoyment is a
Betrayal to my industriousness.
To my belief that anything I put my hand to
Outshines all else.
Such hubris reveals
How vain am I.

Sightseeing From The Train

It's nice to look at backs of houses

Because that's where people seeking fun go.

The backyards not for show.

Extended decks, barbeque pits with

Residue of franks, burgers,

And steaks.

Brick, stick built, ranch and frame,

Semi-detached, quarter plot, half-acre,

And estates.

The backyard's not for show

Because that's where people go to escape.

Tree swings, plastic monkey bars,

Basketball hoops, tennis courts, and pools .

Weedy gardens yielding sweet tomatoes,

Pole beans, pumpkins, berry bushes and

Garden tools.

A rosy arbor that gives sensual joy

A pond with floating lily pads,

And koi.

The backyard's where people seeking peace go.

The backyard's not for show.

An Ocean Of Trees

Reverie

Shifting light between, among, within
Leaves fluttering like waves upon the sea
Misty gray filtering across the denseness
Making a sea-forest from individual trees.

Disappearing horizons lost in rising
Early morning fog spreading fugitively,
Creeping upward to caress the
Tentative blues of Carolina mountain sky and
Coastal sea.

Plunging flashing light striking
Now a bark, now a barn to color it fiery
like a lone burning ship
stuck among the glaring rocks of a raging sea.

Clusters of leaves turned golden, redden, purple.
Deep shadows rising and falling,
Giving the brook a giddy life,
Like breakers upon the shore.

Sullen once more with thirsty clouds wanting
To suck up the golden joy and spread
Gloomy rains splattering on leaves and rocks,
Enclosing all within in a blanket of mist
Creating one solid plane of virtual sea.

About the Author

Janice Peters Sean earned a Ph.D in Education from the University of South Florida, Tampa, and a M.S. in Early Childhood Education from Queens College, CUNY. She has taught students from preschool age to college students for thirty years in New York and Florida. Dr. Sean was born in the Bushwick section of Brooklyn and currently resides in Wilmington, North Carolina. Janice Peters Sean is a watercolor artist and also creates designs for needlepoint canvases.